Where Are Your MANNERS?

Deborah Underwood

Raintree

www.raintreepublishers.co.uk

Visit our website to find out more information about **Raintree** books.

To order:
☎ Phone 44 (0) 1865 888112
📄 Send a fax to 44 (0) 1865 314091
💻 Visit the Raintree bookshop at **www.raintreepublishers.co.uk** to browse our catalogue and order online.

First published in Great Britain by Raintree,
Halley Court, Jordan Hill, Oxford OX2 8EJ,
part of Harcourt Education.
Raintree is a registered trademark of Harcourt
Education Ltd.

Editorial: Louise Galpine and Catherine Veitch
Design: Michelle Lisseter and Bridge Creative Services
Illustrations: Bridge Creative Services
Picture Research: Hannah Taylor and Fiona Orbell
Production: Camilla Crask

Originated by Modern Age
Printed and bound in China by WKT Company
Limited

10-digit ISBN 1 406 20477 3 (hardback)
13-digit ISBN 978 1 4062 0477 3
11 10 09 08 07
10 9 8 7 6 5 4 3 2 1

10-digit ISBN 1 406 20502 8 (paperback)
13-digit ISBN 978 1 4062 0502 2
11 10 09 08 07
10 9 8 7 6 5 4 3 2 1

**British Library Cataloguing in Publication
Data**
Underwood, Deborah
Where are your manners?. - (Fusion)
390
A full catalogue record for this book is available from
the British Library.

Acknowledgements
The publishers would like to thank the following for
permission to reproduce photographs: Corbis pp. **8**
(Steve Raymer), **12–13** (SABA/Tom Wagner), **23**
(Nik Wheeler); Eye Ubiquitous pp. **26–27** (Julia
Waterlow); Getty Images p. **18** (Taxi); Lonely Planet
pp. **4 5** (Greg Elms); Panos pictures pp. **6–7** (Jocelyn
Carlin); Robert Harding pp. **20–21** (Bruno Morandi);
Still Pictures pp. **10–11** (Tom Schulze), **15** (Sebastian
Bolesch), **16–17** (Robert Mulder), **24–25** (Sean
Sprague).

Cover photograph reproduced with permission of
Getty Images (Image Bank).

Every effort has been made to contact copyright
holders of any material reproduced in this book. Any
omissions will be rectified in subsequent printings if
notice is given to the publishers.

The publishers would like to thank Nancy Harris and
Daniel Block for their assistance with the preparation
of this book.

Contents

Some words are printed in bold, **like this**. You can find out what they mean on page 30. You can also look in the box at the bottom of the page where they first appear.

Good morning

Do you behave politely? Do you have good manners? Manners are different around the world. Every country has its own idea about what is polite.

Many people in Japan eat soup and rice for breakfast. They also have fish and pickles. They eat with wooden sticks called **chopsticks**. They sip soup from the bowl.

Children in Japan sleep on **futons**. Futons are thick cloth pads. The pads lie on the floor. In the morning, children fold them up. Then they put them away.

In the Netherlands it is polite to ask others how they slept. Then, it is time for breakfast. Many people enjoy bread with *hagelslag* in the morning. *Hagelslag* is chocolate sprinkles.

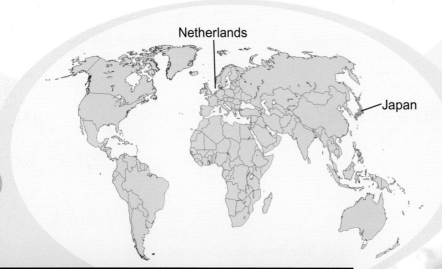

Netherlands

Japan

chopsticks	wooden sticks used to pick up food
futon	thick sleeping pad
hagelslag	chocolate sprinkles

5

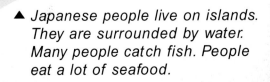

▲ Japanese people live on islands. They are surrounded by water. Many people catch fish. People eat a lot of seafood.

Saying hello

How do you say hello? In some countries it is polite to bow. In other countries people shake hands. What is polite in one place might be rude in another!

In India people say hello with their hands. They put their palms together. Their fingers point up. They may also say *namaste*. This means "I bow to you". Sometimes they greet an **elder** in a special way. An elder is a respected older family member. A younger person sometimes kneels on the ground and touches the elder's feet.

In Tanzania, touching feet means respect, too. People greet elders with the word *shikamoo*. This means "I hold your feet". It is another way to say "I respect you".

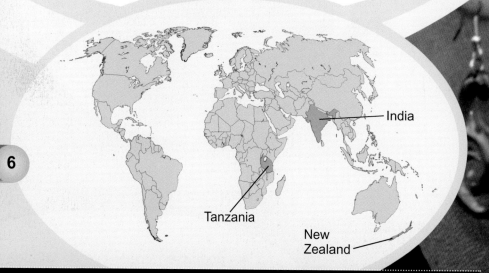

India

Tanzania

New Zealand

elder   respected older family member
hongi   greeting in which two people press their noses together

The Maori live in New Zealand. They greet each other by pressing their noses together. This greeting is called a **hongi**. They may also say *kia ora*. This means "hello".

▼ *Maori greet each other by touching noses.*

In Vietnam people greet ▼ each other by shaking hands or bowing.

Try it!

Talk to a friend. Slowly move closer. When you get too close, does your friend back up? This shows how much personal space your friend needs.

personal space   amount of space people need around them to feel comfortable

Handshakes and hugs

In Vietnam, people often say hello with a small bow. Sometimes they shake hands. In Brazil, friends hug when they meet. Sometimes they kiss each other's cheeks.

Why do people hug in some countries and bow in others? It is partly because they need different amounts of **personal space**. Your personal space is like a bubble around your body. If someone steps inside it, you feel uneasy.

Personal space needs change from country to country. People in Japan might stand more than 90 centimetres (3 feet) apart when they talk. In Egypt people might stand only 25 centimetres (10 inches) apart.

A person who stands too close may seem rude. But he or she may just be from a country where they need less personal space.

Time for school

Now it is time for school. How do you greet your teacher? In many schools in Russia, all the students stand up when the teacher comes in. They stand until the teacher asks them to sit down. They stand again when the teacher leaves. When the teacher asks a question, the student stands up to answer it.

In Russia the first day of school is special. It is called Knowledge Day. It is polite for a young child to bring the teacher flowers.

Russia

Vietnam

School snooze

In Vietnam it is okay to sleep in school! It can be very hot in the middle of the day. In some schools, kids push back their desks. They put mats on the floor. Then they rest or read for two hours.

In Vietnam students do not change rooms for different classes. The teachers change rooms instead. In some schools in the country, it is polite to leave shoes outside the school. This means children go barefoot in class!

▲ *On Knowledge Day Russian children bring their teachers flowers.*

Lunch

Can you hear stomachs growling? It must be time for lunch!

In Japan children eat in their classrooms. They take turns serving lunch. Before they eat, they say *itadakimasu*. This means "I receive". After they eat, they say *gochisosama deshita*. This means "It was a feast"!

Children in Finland never forget their lunch money. They all get free school lunches. After they eat, children take their dishes to the kitchen. Then, they thank the cooks.

In some schools in Finland there are special quiet days. Big red cardboard circles hang on the walls. They remind children not to talk. This makes lunchtime more peaceful.

Burps and slurps

It is okay to slurp your noodles loudly in Japan. It shows that you are enjoying the food. In China it is polite to burp at the table.

13

After school

School is over. It is time to play!

The **Inuit** people in Canada play a game called *muk*. *Muk* means "silence". The children sit in a circle. One goes to the middle and points to someone. That person says *muk*. Then he or she must stay quiet. The person in the middle makes funny faces. If the person who said *muk* laughs, he or she goes to the middle.

Canada

Brazil

Zambia

Try it!

*Children in Brazil play **par ou ímpar**. This means "**even** or **odd**". Put a hand behind your back. Hold up some fingers. Ask a friend to call out "even" or "odd". Show your fingers. Is the number of fingers even or odd? Were they correct?*

even number that can be divided by 2
Inuit native people who live in northern areas
odd number that cannot be divided by 2

▼In Zambia people enjoy the game of *bao*. The game board is made of wood. The pieces are seeds, stones, or marbles. The goal is to take all the other person's pieces.

Happy birthday

No one forgets a birthday in Vietnam. Everybody has the same birthday! Everyone gets one year older on **Tet**. *Tet* is the Vietnamese New Year. On that day adults give children money in red envelopes.

In the days leading up to *Tet*, people clean their houses. But they do not sweep on *Tet*. They believe that would sweep away good luck for the new year.

Say it!

In the Netherlands, *Gefeliciteerd met je verjaardag!* means "Congratulations on your birthday"! People in Vietnam say *Chuc mung nam moi!* It means "Happy New Year"!

Netherlands

Vietnam

Tet Vietnamese New Year

In the Netherlands, the birthday child sits on a fancy chair. The family hangs paper streamers on the chair. People offer good wishes to the whole family. Many people also keep a special birthday calendar. They hang it in the bathroom so they see it all the time. That way they do not forget a birthday.

◀ *In Vietnam everyone celebrates their birthday on New Year's Day. What do you do on your birthday?*

Mexican children ▶
break open objects
called piñatas
at parties. Piñatas
are made from paper
mixed with glue.

Say it!

In Mexico people say ¡Feliz
cumpleaños! instead of "Happy
birthday"! In Finland Hyvää
syntymäpäivää! means "Happy
birthday"!

piñata   hard, hollow object made from paper mixed with glue

Birthday games

Do you like birthday parties? So do children in other countries. They like to play party games with their friends.

Children in Mexico like to break open **piñatas**. A *piñata* is a hard, hollow object. It is filled with sweets. Some *piñatas* look like stars. Others look like animals. They hang from the ceiling. First, children cover their eyes with a blindfold. Then, they take turns hitting the *piñata* with a stick. Finally … crack! The *piñata* breaks open. Sweets spill out. The children dive for them!

In Finland children play a fishing game at parties. It is called *onginta*. An adult hides behind a curtain. Children get a fishing pole with a string and hook. They take turns dropping the string behind the curtain. The adult puts a basket with a prize on the hook. The child fishes out the basket and keeps the prize.

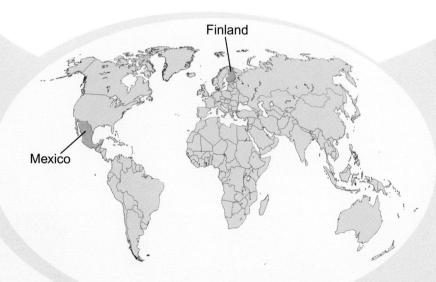

Finland

Mexico

Presents

Most people like getting presents. But be careful what you give! A nice present in one country might be an awful one somewhere else.

The Chinese word for "umbrella" sounds like the word for "break apart". You should not give an umbrella to a new friend in China. They might think you do not want to see them again.

USA

UK

Russia

China

Iran

dozen a group or set of twelve

In China the number four is unlucky. The Chinese word for "four" sounds like the word for "death". It would be bad manners to give someone a set of four things.

Do not give people in Iran yellow flowers. It means you hate them! In the United States and the United Kingdom, people often give a **dozen** roses. But in Russia you must give an **odd** number of flowers. An **even** number is a sign of bad luck.

Visiting

You want to visit some friends. Should you tell them you are coming? In Tanzania it is polite to show up without telling your friends. It is even polite to expect them to feed you. This shows you trust them to take good care of you.

In Japan you take off your shoes when you visit someone's home. You put them in a special place. This place is inside the front door. It is called a **genkan**.

Your host will give you slippers to wear. There are special slippers to wear in the bathroom. It would be very rude to wear the bathroom slippers in other parts of the house.

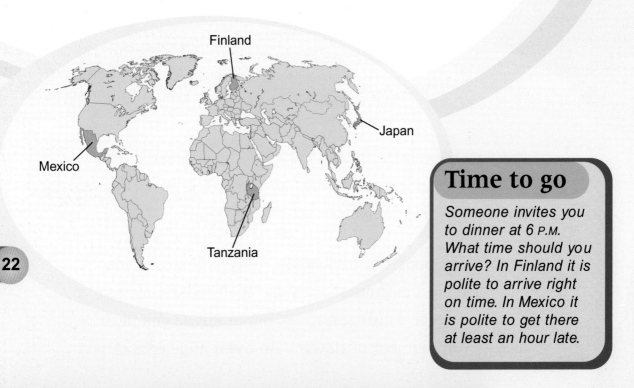

Finland

Japan

Mexico

Tanzania

Time to go

Someone invites you to dinner at 6 P.M. What time should you arrive? In Finland it is polite to arrive right on time. In Mexico it is polite to get there at least an hour late.

genkan   place inside a front door in Japan where shoes are kept

▼ *People in Tanzania enjoy sharing meals with their guests.*

Dinner

Time for dinner! People in India eat with their hands. Many people in India do not eat meat. Dinner might be a lot of small dishes of vegetables. They eat these dishes with rice and bread.

▲ *In some parts of the world, it is good manners to eat with your hands. Is it good manners to do this where you live?*

nshima   ground cooked corn

India

Zambia

People in Zambia eat with their hands, too. They wash their hands at the table. They use a bowl and water jug. Guests wash their hands first. Family members wash next in order of age. The oldest washes first. The youngest washes last.

Zambians eat **nshima** at most meals. *Nshima* is ground corn cooked in water. People roll it into a ball with their hands. Then, they dip the ball into a bowl of cooked food. The food could be meat, fish, or vegetables.

25

Time for bed

The sun sets. It is time to wash and go to sleep. But you still have a chance to use good manners!

Some children in Brazil have a special bed. It is called a **hammock**. Hammocks are made of cloth or net. They hang between two walls or posts. Hammocks can be taken down during the day. That gives people more room in the house. The hammocks swing. Children drift off to sleep.

A Japanese bath is called a *furo*. It is very hot. It is for relaxing. It is not for getting clean. Everyone in the family uses the same bathwater. So it is polite to wash outside the bathtub. People sit by the tub and scrub themselves. A drain in the floor carries away the dirty water.

After a nice long soak, it is time for bed. Children get out their **futons**. Then, they put them on the floor.

Good night!

In Brazil some ▶
children sleep on
hammocks like these.

furo   hot bath
hammock   cloth bed that hangs between two walls or posts

Japan

Brazil

Say it!

In Japan oyasuminasai means "good night"! In Brazil boa noite is "good night".

Manners quiz

Where are your manners?

Looking at manners is a great way to learn about other countries. The different ways people live make the world more interesting. Can you answer these questions?

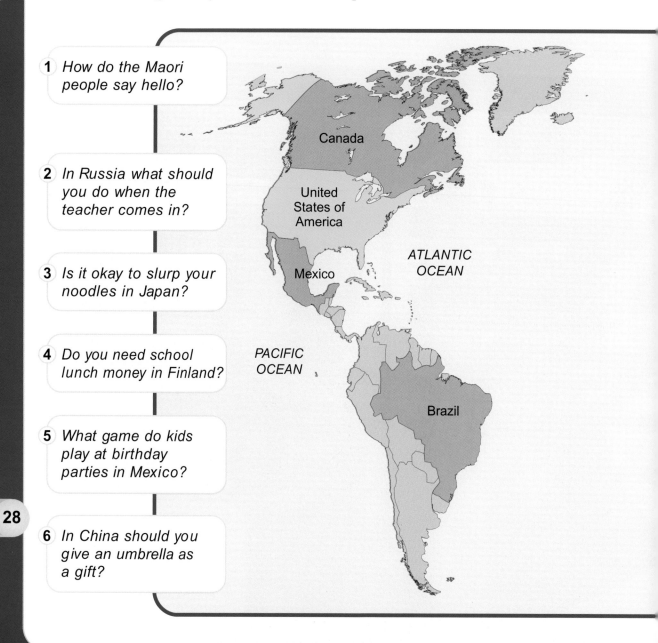

1 How do the Maori people say hello?

2 In Russia what should you do when the teacher comes in?

3 Is it okay to slurp your noodles in Japan?

4 Do you need school lunch money in Finland?

5 What game do kids play at birthday parties in Mexico?

6 In China should you give an umbrella as a gift?

Canada

United States of America

Mexico

ATLANTIC OCEAN

PACIFIC OCEAN

Brazil

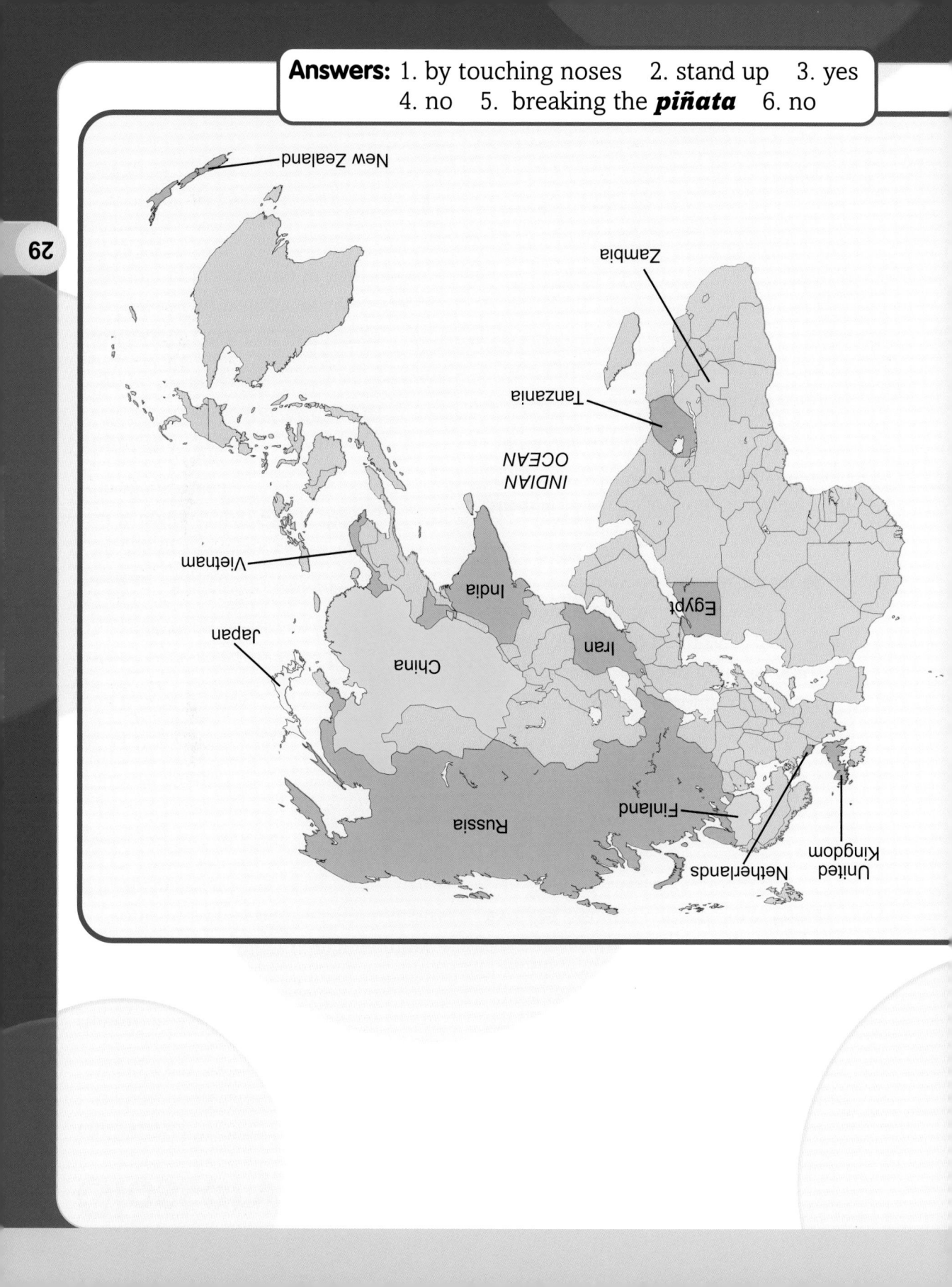

Answers: 1. by touching noses   2. stand up   3. yes
4. no   5. breaking the *piñata*   6. no

Glossary

chopsticks wooden sticks used to pick up food. Chinese and Japanese people eat with chopsticks.

dozen a group or set of twelve. Roses are often sold as a dozen.

elder respected older family member. People in some countries greet elders in special ways.

even number that can be divided by 2. The numbers 2, 4, 6, 8, and 10 are even.

furo hot bath. People in Japan soak in a *furo* to relax.

futon thick sleeping pad. Japanese people sleep on futons.

genkan place inside a front door in Japan where shoes are kept. It is polite to leave your shoes in the *genkan*.

hagelslag chocolate sprinkles. Dutch people eat *hagelslag* on bread for breakfast.

hammock cloth bed that hangs between two walls or posts. Some people in Brazil sleep in hammocks.

hongi greeting in which two people press their noses together. The Maori people greet each other with a *hongi*.

Inuit native people who live in northern areas. The Inuit play a game called *muk*.

nshima ground cooked corn. People in Zambia eat *nshima* for almost every meal.

odd number that cannot be divided by 2. The numbers 1, 3, 5, 7, and 9 are odd.

personal space amount of space people need around them to feel comfortable. In countries where people greet each other with a hug and kiss, they do not need a lot of personal space.

piñata hard, hollow object made from paper mixed with glue. Breaking the *piñata* is a popular game in Mexico.

Tet Vietnamese New Year. All people in Vietnam celebrate their birthdays on *Tet*.

Want to know more?

Books to read

- *A Life Like Mine*, Amanda Rayner (Dorling Kindersley, 2002)

- *Birthdays Around the World*, Mary D. Lankford (HarperCollins, 2002)

- *Let's Eat!: Children and Their Food Around the World*, Beatrice Hollyer (Oxfam, 2003)

Jet off around the world in ***World's Wonders***. Take a good look at Earth's landforms. There are high places, low places, wet places, and dry places. Where would you like to go?

Find out how people communicated with each other in the past in ***Did You Hear the News?***

Index